"In addition to coming up with the most creative ways to raise children, Silvana Clark has the unique ability to write an entertaining book that stimulates and inspires everyone else to be just as creative . . . or at least to try!

Learning lessons while growing up *can* be fun, and all it takes are examples from Silvana to kick-start our own creativity. This book is a must-have for every parent (and grandparent!) who has been either frustrated or bored with family routine. Nothing about the Clarks is routine, and that's worth imitating!"

—Cindy Groom-Harry, Craft Marketing Connections, Inc.,
author, designer, and television personality

"*Stuffed Animals on the Ceiling Fan*, like its author, Silvana Clark, is a treasure not to be taken lightly. Read the book and remember the creative power that overflows when we loosen up, laugh, and enjoy the moments."

Barbara Brock, Re.D., professor of Recreation Management,
Eastern Washington University, author

"Silvana's approach and writing style helps parents know that they are not alone—and that there is no magic template to child rearing success. Each child will reveal a series of surprises. We truly enjoyed reading this book."

Jim and Pam Behling, founders and directors of Deer Creek
Adventure Camp, Medina, Texas

Stuffed Animals on the Ceiling Fan

And Other Off-the-Wall Parenting
Techniques that Really Work

Silvana Clark

Fleming H. Revell
A Division of Baker Book House Co
Grand Rapids, Michigan 49516

Published by Fleming H. Revell
a division of Baker Book House Company
P.O. Box 6287, Grand Rapids, MI 49516-6287
www.bakerbooks.com

Printed in the United States of America

Library of Congress Cataloging-in-Publication Data

Clark, Silvana.
   Stuffed animals on the ceiling fan : and other off-the-wall parenting techniques that really work / Silvana Clark.
      p.   cm.
  ISBN 0-8007-5842-0 (pbk.)
   1. Parenting—Religious aspects—Christianity. 2. Child rearing—Religious aspects—Christianity. I. Title.
BV4526.3 .C57 2003
649′ .1—dc21   2002012781

Scripture is taken from the HOLY BIBLE, NEW INTERNATIONAL VERSION®. NIV®. Copyright © 1973, 1978, 1984 by International Bible Society. Used by permission of Zondervan. All rights reserved.

Contents

Introduction: Not a Traditional Parenting
Book   7

Part 1   Family Fun and Frivolity   11
         Along with Downright Silliness
Part 2   Raising Self-Confident Children   49
         Who Are Not Arrogant or Conceited
Part 3   Getting Chores Completed   75
         Even Though They Are Not Quite Up to House
         Beautiful *Standards*
Part 4   Creating Family Traditions   99
         Howl at the Moon and Collect Souvenir Rocks
Part 5   Dealing with the Mundane Aspects
         of Life   129
         *Bedtime, Meals, Shopping, Cleaning the Lint
         Trap*

Conclusion   190

Introduction
Not a Traditional Parenting Book

Remember how you devoured parenting books when your child was a newborn? You frantically researched every aspect of infant care, from how to clean her belly button to cutting her tiny fingernails. As a new parent, you depended on the advice of experienced parents . . . parents with babies at least three months older than yours. Sometimes it seemed like the experts had all the answers, while you floundered in your parenting skills.

Eventually, all parents develop their own style of parenting, adjusted to fit the needs of their particular children. Traditional parenting tips provide the groundwork to raise happy, confident children. Then reality hits: the traditional parenting tip doesn't fit your particular personality or the needs of your child. That's when you know drastic measures need to be taken to make an impact on your child. You resort to "parental reality," the highly creative and innovative technique of doing something totally outrageous to catch your child off guard.

When our older daughter Trina got her first job working in a deli, we wanted to observe her at work. "Please don't let me see you at the deli," she told us as she left for her first day on the job. She didn't see *us,* that's for sure. How could she recognize us when we were decked out in clever disguises? My husband looked dashing in his plaid sports coat, slicked-back hair, pirate eye patch, and top hat perched on his head. I wore a curly red wig left over from a production of *Annie,* along with a Superman cape over my silver jumpsuit. And who would have recognized our two-year-old, wearing the plastic Groucho Marx glasses and mustache? Trina obviously pretended not to notice us, while we got to observe her at work and even snap a few clandestine pictures. You won't find that tip in a traditional parenting book.

When our daughter Sondra was born, we soon learned traditional parenting tips weren't going to work. At only three hours old, she was "kicked out" of the baby nursery because she cried so much she disturbed the other angelic babies. A polite way of describing her was "an active-alert child." My only goal each day was to keep her physically active. During the winter, that meant joining the senior citizen mall walkers for several hours every morning. I'd follow my toddler from one end of the mall to the other as she waved to all her grandma and grandpa friends. On most days, she wore her dance leotard with a flouncy square-dance petticoat and tap shoes. (They made a delightful clicking sound on the mall floor.)

While being potty trained, Sondra fell in love with a pair of silky underpants. They were too beautiful to cover the traditional part of her body, so she wore them on her head. This way, according to her logic, as she walked the mall in her petticoat and tap shoes, everyone could see and feel the silky fabric on her head if they wanted. When she was five, I walked into her Sunday school class to see her standing on a table, performing a monologue called "The Ugly Stepsister" in which she describes life in the shadow of Cinderella. The teacher came over to me, holding back tears of laughter. "You'll never believe what she did this time," she said. "I admit, I wasn't that prepared today, so we sang more songs than usual. Finally Sondra told me she thought we needed a change of pace from all the singing and she would help pass the time by performing a monologue."

Sondra never feel asleep before 11:00 P.M. yet woke up at 6:00 A.M., chattering about her plans for the day. My husband and I tried many traditional tips but soon learned to trust our own judgment and feel the freedom to be creative. Today, as a twelve-year-old, Sondra has published four books, appeared regularly on television shows, and raised thirty-five thousand dollars last year for Childcare International, a Christian relief organization. Who knows, maybe one day researchers will discover the key to success results from wearing underwear on your head!

Stuffed Animals on the Ceiling Fan provides a balance between commonsense parenting tips and what real-life parents do in real-life situations. Some of the ideas might be a bit unorthodox, but they demonstrate the creativity parents use in raising their children. Albert Einstein said,

"Imagination is more important than knowledge." When parents demonstrate innovative parenting techniques, children will learn how to develop their own unique ways of problem solving. In a study of one hundred CEOs of Fortune 500 companies, the CEOs were asked, "What two characteristics do you look for in selecting employees?" They answered: 1) creativity, 2) intelligence. These professionals felt it was more important to be able to develop new and creative ideas than to be members of Mensa without creativity.

In *Stuffed Animals on the Ceiling Fan,* you'll discover innovative ideas from parents like yourself. You'll meet parents who serve Poached Lizard Lips for dinner, cut the cord of their television sets, and give their children "Get out of Bed Free" cards. Oh, yes. You'll also read traditional and helpful hints on keeping kids occupied on car trips and how to make chores palatable.

Most of all, this book is a tribute to parents who love their children and want to see them grow into confident, productive members of society. If that means being a little silly or untraditional, then so be it. As you read this book, consider the traditional parenting tips as helpful hints to deal with your child. While reading "What Parents *Really* Do," laugh and learn from other parents.

Part 1

Family Fun and Frivolity
(Along with Downright Silliness)

Parents have a tendency to take their parenting role seriously—too seriously. The following ideas demonstrate the importance of letting loose and simply enjoying the fun of childhood.

Ever Play "Giggle and Spit"?

Traditional Parenting Tip

We've all heard, "The family that plays together, stays together." As families get frazzled racing from one activity to another, it's important to regularly spend time at home together, casually playing games and eating popcorn. If Monopoly seems too long and too involved, try playing a simple card game or charades. Some families play intricate games of hide-and-seek, going so far as to rearrange closets ahead of time to create the perfect hiding place. Let family members take turns deciding on a fifteen-minute daily activity. You could find yourself simply throwing a Frisbee or building a fort out of couch cushions. The preschooler in your family might suggest repeating what he experienced in preschool—finger painting on the table with chocolate pudding!

What Parents **Really** Do

Okay, I admit it. One of our favorite games is "Giggle and Spit." Doesn't the name alone make you want to play? Each player gets a glass of water and a washcloth. One person, selected to be "it," stands in front of the group. Everyone (except "it") takes a big gulp of water and holds it in their mouth. "It" begins making goofy faces or telling jokes, trying to make everyone else laugh and spit out the water—usually through their nose. That's why you have washcloths. Most children can be reduced to hysterical laughter when a parent simply whispers in a dramatic voice, "poopy diapers."

"Giggle and Spit" champion of Florida

Traditional Parenting Tip

Help children develop a playful, creative outlook toward life. Jesus promises us "abundant life." If your kids know the basic rules of proper behavior, let loose in other areas. Encourage untraditional thinking. "What would be the wildest, craziest thing we can do on Saturday that doesn't cost over five dollars?" "Who can make up a game using this badminton racket and a balloon?" Let family members know it's great to think in creative ways.

What Parents **Really** Do

Catherine had a problem getting her son, Tommy, to eat breakfast. No matter what she tried, he just wouldn't eat typical breakfast foods such as cereal, eggs, toast, waffles, and pancakes. When Tommy was ready to start kindergarten, Catherine decided to try a new approach. Finally, she stumbled onto chicken soup and pastina, which Tommy loved and ate for breakfast every day.

Even as an adult, Tommy continued to have chicken soup and pastina for breakfast, although not every day. It's no wonder that Tommy later became Tom Lagana—coauthor of the books *Chicken Soup for the Volunteer's Soul* and *Chicken Soup for the Prisoner's Soul*.

Tom Lagana, coauthor of *Chicken Soup for the Volunteer's Soul* and *Chicken Soup for the Prisoner's Soul*

Traditional Parenting Tip

Aah, the day every parent dreams of: your child is going away to sleepover camp—a whole week where someone else entertains and supervises your child! To make camp a positive experience, try these hints:

- A few days before camp begins, send a post-card so it arrives at mail call on the first day of camp.
- Check with the camp director ahead of time to see if parents can send candy and treats. Some camps place restrictions on candy in cabins.
- Have your child earn his/her own money ahead of time to spend in the camp store.
- When selecting a camp, ask about the return rate for campers. When campers and siblings come back year after year, it's a good sign the camp is well run.

Let your child have a say in selecting the camp. You might be leaning toward a camp heavy on sports skills while your son simply wants to learn how to build model rockets. Children are more enthusiastic about camp if they take part in the selection process.

What Parents **Really** Do

As a former camp counselor, I know how camps make a big deal about mail call. Sometimes the camper getting the most mail has to sing a silly song or some other "penance." I prefer to simply embarrass my son at camp. I send him postcards with messages such as "I miss you so much," or "You have the cutest eyebrows I've ever seen." I make sure to draw hearts and lips all over the postcard so it catches the counselor's attention during mail call. Dousing the postcard with perfume is another nice touch.

Former counselor "Laughing Squirrel"

Less Is Sometimes Better

Traditional Parenting Tip

A report in *Affirmative Parenting* magazine (John Rosemond, "Too Many Toys?" winter 2001–2002, p. 19) gave a startling statistic. By the time children are five years old, they'll have consumed 250 toys. That's fifty toys per year, or about one a week. Why do children need so many "things"? No wonder they rip through stacks of presents on their birthday and ask, "Is that all?" Make a conscious effort to cut back on toys for your children. Encourage them to use what they already have. Some parents incorporate a policy of discarding or donating two "old" toys for every new toy brought in the house.

What Parents **Really** Do

It seemed like every week my kids were bringing home those colorful flyers advertising school book clubs. Sure, the prices were reasonable, but my kids were under the impression we'd buy as many books as they wanted, simply because they were connected with school. We worked out a plan. They could order three books—which they paid for out of their own money. After the books arrived and they had read them (or said they read them), we'd quiz them on the book. If it was obvious they really had read the book, we'd buy it back from them, giving them money for the next order sheet. It amazed me how they suddenly became very selective about ordering books.

"Book Warden" in Seattle with three children

Giving the Gift of Play

Traditional Parenting Tip

Bedtime, devotions, nutritious meals, teaching manners . . . it's overwhelming what parents do each day. In the rush of taking care of necessities, we forget the art of having fun. Silly parents enjoying a good laugh with their children goes a long way toward creating family harmony. Play a game of hide-and-seek before bedtime. Celebrate the cat's birthday. Eat dinner in the kid's bedroom. Bring home some origami paper and laugh because your paper cranes look more like paper buffalos. Stand against the outside of the house and try not to flinch as family members toss wet sponges near your face. The main point is to create that warm feeling of closeness that develops after sharing fun together.

What Parents **Really** Do

One thing I have done with nieces, nephews, and now my own son is play "Washer and Dryer." I pick up the child, twist back and forth, and tell the child, "You're being washed." Then the spin cycle, followed by rinse, and another spin. Finally, a brief "tumble dry." They learn how their clothes get washed and laugh and giggle as well. Eventually, Uncle/Dad needs to stop—the "washer/dryer" does tire easily!

John L. Hoh Jr.

21

Bubble-Blowing Bonanza

Traditional Parenting Tip

Teachers are known for having quick educational activities on hand when children need a break from the ordinary routine. You'll have a ready supply of ideas for family fun if you collect magazine articles or invest in a few books on family activities. Keep a stash of homemade bubble solution handy for those times when children need a quick activity.

Bubble Solution

Mix together 6 cups water with 1/2 cup dishwashing detergent (Joy and Dawn work best). Add 1/2 tablespoon glycerin (available in drugstores) and mix well. Let sit overnight.

Experiment with wire coat hangers, flyswatters, and other objects to get the maximum bubbles. Try blowing bubbles at night while someone shines a flashlight on them. If you're very clever, trap bubbles on a flat surface and watch what happens if you carefully put them in the freezer.

What Parents **Really** Do

Forget dyeing two dozen eggs at Easter and hiding them. What fun is it to go on an egg hunt and find only a few eggs? We buy bags of peanuts in their shells and hide hundreds in the yard. A few are specially marked to be exchanged for prizes. Everyone loves finding handfuls of peanuts. We used to hide miniature Tootsie Rolls. Now we have more fun hiding the peanuts, knowing the squirrels enjoy the leftovers. This has become a tradition at all family gatherings. We've even had our peanut hunt in the snow at our New Year's Eve party.

Former flight attendant, now professional peanut hider

Traditional Parenting Tip

Christian Hageseth, author of *A Laughing Place*, wrote, "Humor is the single best antidote for parent burnout." Humor plays a central role in parent/child attachment. Some parents adopt the "ASAP" philosophy of parenting—"As Silly as Possible." In fact, the word *silly* is derived from the Old English word (ge)sælig, which means to be completely happy, blessed. The next time your child irritates you, look for the humor in the situation. Teach children the value of laughing and being blessed by being silly. (Okay, you'll probably need a short lesson on why you shouldn't be silly during communion; but then again, maybe *after* communion is all right. Some parents actually take home the used communion cups, wash them out, and let kids use them for craft projects.)

What Parents **Really** <u>Really</u> Do

I took this idea from the menu of a restaurant that was always packed with families. To make our stay-at-home, Friday-night-leftover dinners memorable, I'd print out a menu. It might include "Poached Lizard Lips, Fried Frog Feet, and Raw Brussels Sprouts." The kids were so glad to actually get "regular" food, they didn't mind eating leftovers.

Home schooling mom with four children

"Out of the Box" Family Adventures

Traditional Parenting Tip

Ever feel your family is in a rut? Carve out time to expose your children to new experiences. Is there a traveling gospel choir coming to town? Check it out. Does your community offer a children's parade? Get busy and design a float out of an old refrigerator box. If your family is actively involved in sports, branch out and see a local production of *The Nutcracker* ballet. Attend a different church and compare styles of worship. Children benefit from seeing people involved in a wide range of experiences. Local newspapers often carry calendars of upcoming events. Be bold and take your family on a new adventure.

What Parents **Really** Do

For several days, a group of local college students staged a protest in our downtown area. They wanted a piece of property turned into a community park instead of a new office building. The "Pit Protesters," as they called themselves, attached bicycle locks around their necks and connected themselves to a tall sculpture in the middle of the pit. Several others built seats on the sculpture and perched on chairs twenty feet in the air. Since I knew they weren't dangerous, I told Sondra we were going on a "Before School Breakfast Adventure." We drove to the area and walked around, looking at the creativity of the protesters. Police couldn't arrest them because they were attached to the metal pole! Sondra and I ate a bagel breakfast across the street from the pit and had a great conversation about the right to protest for what you believe in. Sure beats eating cereal at home.

Silvana

Singin' in the Rain

Traditional Parenting Tip

Do your children own rubber boots? Do you have an umbrella? Then why not use them? All too often, parents display their serious personality and say, "You'll have to stay inside. It's raining." Unless there's a major lightning storm, why let a little rain stop the fun? Gather up boots and umbrellas and go for a rain walk. No raincoats? Cut head and armholes in a large trash bag and put it on. (Don't worry about the neighbors. They'll enjoy watching the trash bag parade.) Stick out your tongues and catch raindrops. Link arms and sing a rousing chorus of "Singin' in the Rain." Try a gentle jog for even more exercise. You'll feel better and your children will release pent-up energy. Ever consider being artistic with rain? Sprinkle dry tempera paint on a piece of cardboard. Go outside and let the rain splatter the paint to make a colorful picture.

What Parents **Really** Do

My three- and five-year-old get cabin fever. So when it rains, sometimes we put on boots and go puddle stomping. The girls jump from puddle to puddle, come home, and take a great nap.

Tamara Rogers, mother of three

Special Activities for a Special Family

Traditional Parenting Tip

Teach children the meaning of the word *special*. Use special dishes on birthdays or celebratory events. Put fresh flowers and candles on the table to create a special atmosphere for their macaroni and cheese. Every family member should have one set of special clothes to wear to weddings and church. The idea is to add an element of distinction, to set aside the ordinary in order to enjoy the extraordinary. Why have an ordinary bath? It becomes a special time with scented bubbles, candles, and a snack.

What Parents **Really** Do

My mother had a special box of "indoor toys" that we could only play with when it rained. It included a spin art set and some unusual board games. We actually liked rainy days. My mother passed away when I was ten. We started playing with the indoor toys all the time, and we lost interest in them within a few weeks.

Margaret Martin, parks and recreation director

Spouse Fun = Family Fun

Traditional Parenting Tip

We've often heard, "The best thing parents can do for their children is love each other." It's true. Parents who display a healthy relationship toward each other become positive role models for their children. Children observe the subtle nuances of communication and displays of affection. Try to spend quality time (even a short amount of time) with your spouse on a daily basis. One couple watched the evening news together, holding hands. Their kids left them alone since they weren't interested in the news.

What Parents **Really** Do

All the parenting books tell parents how important it is to spend quality time together without children around. We had a limited budget and few relatives in the area to baby-sit. So on Friday nights, we'd rent a video and put an old shower curtain on the floor. Sound romantic? We'd fill our toddler's small plastic wading pool with water and let him "swim" in the middle of the living room. We'd watch the movie, occasionally adding warm water to the pool, while he played happily for over an hour. Then we put our wrinkled prune to bed.

Creative new parents from Dallas

Less TV, More Family Fun

Traditional Parenting Tip

Parents often admit their family watches too much television. Rather than just complaining, take positive action. Announce at breakfast, "Tonight we're starting a new game night." At breakfast, display the ingredients for homemade play dough. Children can look forward to mixing the ingredients and making squishy clay dinosaurs after dinner. Instead of simply declaring "No TV," provide fun alternatives. A survey by *Weekly Reader* asked fifteen hundred children, "What makes a happy family?" The number one answer? "Doing things together."

What Parents **Really** Do

Since we watch very little TV, I frequently plan evening family activities. One afternoon, a few days before Halloween, I set up an indoor carnival in our living room. Within twenty minutes I had eight "booths" set up. You could toss wadded up socks into a wastebasket or roll marbles into a shoe box for points. If that wasn't enough excitement, you could play "Pin the Nose on the Pumpkin" or toss a Frisbee through a hoop. For the next three days, Sondra wanted to "do the booths" every night. When her friends came over on Halloween, they spent another half hour playing the carnival games. One girl said, "This is *so* much fun. I can't believe I'm throwing a Frisbee *inside* a house."

Silvana

Limiting Tube Time

Traditional Parenting Tip

L imiting children's time watching TV or playing on the computer is an ongoing battle. Try some of these tips:

- Allocate ten dimes to each child weekly. Each dime can be traded in for fifteen minutes of computer or TV time. (Most kids would rather keep the money.)
- Put the TV in the basement or a storage room so it's uncomfortable to watch.
- Declare school nights to be TV-free nights.
- Set a good example by not watching TV every night after the kids are in bed.

What Parents **Really** Do

My kids are quick to bring snacks and toys into the rec room where they watch TV or play with the computer. We have a new rule: The rec room has to be clean before the TV or computer can be turned on. If a child really has a show he wants to watch, he'll clean up. Most often they go outside and play rather than bother with cleaning up yesterday's mess.

TV-free mom

No Chance to Be Bored

Traditional Parenting Tip

Watch TV for more than an hour and you'll see a show or commercial where children state, "I'm soooo bored." This reinforces the concept to your children. It becomes acceptable to complain about boredom. Children today feel the need to be entertained at all times. Let them figure out what to do when "there's nothing to do." Ahead of time, sit down with your children and have each make a list of "what I can do when I have free time." They can list activities from reading to making fairy houses from twigs to learning origami. Be sure to include: "Have Mom assign some cleaning chores." Hang the list on the refrigerator. Then, when children complain about boredom, put a cheerful smile on your face and point to the list. If they continue complaining, repeat step 1: Put a cheerful smile on your face and point to the list (particularly the part about the chores). They'll soon get busy doing something.

What Parents **Really** Do

The words "I'm bored" or anything related to those words are forbidden. If I hear that word, the kids have immediate chores.

Shelly Brown

Twenty More Hours a Week

Traditional Parenting Tip

More Americans own a TV set than have indoor plumbing. An even more sobering thought is that most grade-school children watch over twenty hours of television each week. That's equivalent to a part-time job! Instead of watching TV, insist your children add to the household income by working at Denny's. Maybe that's not possible, but think about the creative possibilities for an extra twenty hours a week. Could your children use some of that time to learn a new hobby? What if the family sat down and spent even one hour a night playing games or putting together a puzzle? The memories of family fun last much longer than a rerun of *Who Wants to Be a Millionaire*.

What Parents **Really** Do

I'd had it. I tried bribes, nagging, and forbidding—yet still my kids were glued to the TV. In frustration, I made a dramatic gesture of waving scissors in front of them and saying, "See these scissors? They cut things. They cut things like TV cords. Watch this." I turned off the TV, unplugged it, and then quickly cut off the plug.

Mommy Scissorhands

S-T-R-E-T-C-H-I-N-G the Rules

Traditional Parenting Tip

Children benefit from consistent rules and expectations. Some things, like wearing a bike helmet or being kind to animals, are simply nonnegotiable. Yet occasionally bending some rules teaches children to adjust to different situations. Not every rule carries the same importance. Why shouldn't the birthday girl get to eat ice cream for breakfast? What's wrong with sleeping in the living room on a Friday night? Before automatically saying "no" to a request, be open to other considerations. One family found that Sundays took on a whole new meaning of family togetherness when their daughter suggested attending their church's Saturday evening service instead. Sunday became the one day of the week that everyone stayed home.

What Parents **Really** Do

You'll have no problem getting your boys to take baths if you let them bring with them the frogs they caught earlier in the ditch.

Linda Smit, home schooling mom

Traditional Parenting Tip

"A cheerful heart is good medicine" (Proverbs 17:22). In other words, look at the bright side of life. We often wonder why our children are so negative, yet we may be sending that very message. Have you ever heard yourself say, "My boss is so unfair," or "I'll never learn that new computer program"? Tell your children they can fine you ten cents for every negative statement you make next weekend. Then do the same with them the following week. Who ends up with the most money? Many businesses now hire high-priced consultants to teach employees how to have fun. It seems employees are so stressed from balancing their personal and professional lives that they need "experts" to teach them to have fun. Give your children a head start in the business world by putting fun into daily routines. Write "I love you" on the mirror with lipstick. Include silly jokes in their lunch bags.

What Parents **Really** Do

In our house, if someone moans and groans and complains, we all gather around that person and yell, in unison, "Hey, Buddy—that's stinking thinking!"

Positive Pauline

45

Traditional Parenting Tip

The media is constantly telling us about the rise in Type II diabetes in children caused by obesity. As soon as your little one can toddle, look for opportunities to let her exercise. If waiting for a flight at the airport, why confine your child? Walk to the farthest point of the airport and back. Then hit the other end of the terminal. Can you walk to school with your child occasionally? Nothing like starting the day with a two-mile jaunt. (Think how the exercise will benefit both of you.) Park at the farthest end of the parking lot at the mall. Every bit of exercise is beneficial for the entire family.

What Parents **Really** Do

When Sondra was a toddler, my first thought every morning was, "Thank you, God, for the possibility of a new day." The second thought was, "What can I do to 'wear out' Sondra?" On rainy days, we'd join the senior citizen mall walkers. She'd race from one end of the mall to another, waving to elderly walkers and saying "hi" and "bye." I'd follow her for over an hour on a nonstop journey. Every day, rain or shine, we'd hike the 3/4-mile "Poop Loop" trail behind our house. We'd take two dogs and two sheep. (That explains the name of the trail.) We seldom used a stroller in order to let her walk and run as much as possible. Many other times, the cemetery became a peaceful place to let her run loose.

Silvana

Part 2

Raising Self-Confident Children (Who Are Not Arrogant or Conceited)

As parents, we want our children to be able to express their opinions and overcome challenges. Discover how parents raise self-confident children with a positive outlook on life.

Take a Tip from Monopoly

Traditional Parenting Tip

Kevin Leman, Ph.D. and family marriage therapist, sees many parents complaining about a strong-willed child. "He challenges everything I say," exclaim frustrated parents. Dr. Leman encourages parents to give children positive outlets for excess energy. Practice jogging together for a road run. Play Frisbee in the front yard. Most of all, give children more control of their lives. Let them see they can make age-appropriate choices. When children feel responsible for themselves, they have less reason to confront parental authority.

What Parents **Really** Do

Our family loves playing Monopoly Jr. I use this interest to help take the ordeal out of bedtime. Every Sunday my kids each receive three "Get out of Bed Free" cards, which I designed on the computer. Throughout the week, if they get out of bed for some frivolous reason, they have to turn in one of their cards. Any cards left over the following Sunday can be redeemed for fifty cents each. Now, they stay in bed, knowing it's worth an extra $1.50. The money is worth it to me for a hassle-free bedtime.

"I love Boardwalk" dad

Creative Problem Solving

Traditional Parenting Tip

Because teachers see so many students unable to make simple decisions, many schools now offer problem solving as part of their curriculum. "Tell me what to do," some children ask. They're scared to make choices for fear they'll do the wrong thing. Begin your own problem-solving program when children are young. If they complain about a problem, have them make a list of possible solutions. Throw in a few silly ideas just to stretch their imagination. After all, selling your wedding ring *is* one way your son could get money for a new bike. Teach children to be creative in solving problems.

What Parents **Really** Do

Our daughter was having trouble with fractions. Somehow, multiplying 1/4 and 2/3 made no sense to her. My ever-resourceful husband came to the rescue: "Trina, let's make cookies! Then you can see how fractions produce a great treat." I entered the kitchen an hour later to find cookies and cookie dough on every piece of available counter space. He certainly had taught Trina to multiply fractions. He gave her the original recipe and had her *quadruple* it!

Silvana, wife of Allan, mathematician extraordinaire

Traditional Parenting Tip

New situations produce stress for some children. What does it mean when you say, "Be good at Aunt Cindy's wedding"? They may not remember who Aunt Cindy is, let alone how to be good at a wedding. Explain what to expect before children get in unfamiliar situations. If you're visiting a friend in the hospital, talk about the strong smells they'll encounter, or the nurses with cloth face masks. If your child is taking his first plane ride, set up rows of chairs and demonstrate why he can't kick the seat in front of him or repeatedly push the flight attendant call button. (Although it is great fun to watch them come running when you push the button.) Are you heading out to a "fancy" restaurant? Discuss the difference between eating at McDonald's and La Fancy-Shmancy restaurant.

What Parents **Really** Do

A friend with two young boys visited us recently and our two families went out to a nice restaurant. My friend's boys became more and more boisterous. Finally, my friend shouted "quiet" at the top of his lungs. You could hear a pin drop in the entire restaurant.

John Holland, recreation director

Take That Risk!

Traditional Parenting Tip

Even if you are shy yourself, encourage children to take part in life, rather than merely observe. We've all heard that there are three types of people in life:

1. Some people make things happen.
2. Some people watch things happen.
3. Some people say, "What happened?"

Set an example by taking appropriate risks yourself. Tell your children how you took on a new project at work. Offer to decorate the Sunday school bulletin board at church. Call the radio station if you know the answer to their trivia contest. Why be a bystander in life when there are so many fulfilling opportunities available? Show your children how to take control of life and make things happen.

What Parents **Really** Do

We've taught our kids to be "front-row" kids. Whenever we go to a play, we try to sit as close as possible to the front. "It's fun to see the actors' faces," I tell my kids. "Sometimes you can see the spit coming out of their mouths." At church, you'll find us up front where we can see the flowers or check out the pastor's socks. Now that habit has transferred to our kids at school, where they sit at the front of the class. They have fewer distractions and the teachers call on them often. Oh, yes, sometimes they even see a drop of spit coming out of their teacher's mouth.

Front-row mama

Time for Time-Out

Traditional Parenting Tip

For most children, each day is open-ended with possibilities. It's only adults who say, "Hurry up—it's ten minutes until church," or "Get ready, the bus comes in five minutes." To a six-year-old, there's little difference between ten minutes and two hours. Some children understand time in relation to TV. "We'll drive to the dentist's this afternoon. The ride is as long as one cartoon." Experts also suggest setting appropriate time limits for the all-important "time-out." Since young children have such a limited concept of time, set a time-out of one minute for every year of the child. A three-year-old sits for three minutes. (Although when they're screaming and kicking the whole time, three minutes may seem like three months!)

What Parents Really Do

To help my children gain an awareness of time, we play "games" relating to various amounts of time. I might say, "I'm setting the timer. For the next five minutes everyone has to run around the outside of the house until the timer goes off." Sometimes, when we're outside on a summer day, one person has to talk about himself for sixty seconds straight. If he stops talking before fifty seconds, or goes over one minute, we dump a glass of water on his head.

Dad with a stopwatch

The Art of Brainstorming

Traditional Parenting Tip

Teach children techniques of brainstorming to solve problems. It's all too easy to complain, "I'll never learn to tie my shoes," or "Nobody likes me at school." When children have a problem, help them brainstorm possible solutions. If some of the ideas are a bit off-the-wall, that's okay. At least the ideas are flowing. Ask them, "What's the worst thing that could happen in this situation? How would you handle that? If you had a magic wand, how would you change this situation?" By encouraging limitless possibilities, children see more than one option. They might never become the most popular person at school, but they can develop a core group of close friends. Maybe they lack the flexibility needed to be a competitive gymnast, but they can be a standout in community drama. When stuck for ideas about a particular situation, ask your children to list possible solutions.

What Parents **Really** Do

We worked out a great win-win situation with three young children at dinner. Cooking became a complex juggling contest with pots and pans, temper tantrums, and a frustrated mom. Our elderly neighbor used to be a teacher and has tons of great flannel-board stories and art projects. On Tuesdays and Thursdays, she comes over for forty-five minutes to play with my kids while I make dinner. Then she eats with us. She enjoys being part of a family, and I certainly enjoy making dinner in peace.

Mom who enjoys some carefree cooking

Saying Yes

Traditional Parenting Tip

Don't be afraid to bend the rules in low-level decisions. Does it really matter if your son's pajama top and bottom match? What's wrong with your daughter asking to eat her broccoli raw instead of cooked? We're all too quick to tell our children no. Save the absolutes for major issues such as wearing bicycle helmets or attending church. "Mom, I know it's raining, but can Jason and I eat our snack outside *under* the picnic table?" Why not? If children see your flexibility in day-to-day situations, they'll be more likely to abide by your firm decisions on major issues.

What Parents **Really** Do

When my son Ryan was a preschooler, he absolutely loved our Christmas tree. He'd touch the ornaments, asking me to explain where each one came from. The colored lights fascinated him, so he'd gently move them around. When it was time to take the tree down in late December, he was crushed. How could we remove his beloved tree? We'd even slept by it on Christmas Eve. I ignored the dropping needles. We kept the tree up for several more weeks, even going so far as to add silver streamers and party hats on New Year's. Finally, after a festive Valentine party, our red-doily-covered tree came down.

Betty Olson, mother of Ryan, who is now a doctor

Children Are Roses

Traditional Parenting Tip

A poster showing a bouquet of roses stated:

Roses have thorns, or
Thorns have roses.
How do you see life?

Do you see your child as a rose—or bristling with thorns? Of course it would be wonderful if your son were as talented, kind, cute, musical, athletic, and brilliant as little Johnny next door. Look at the positive characteristics of your children. Is she a risk taker? Great, she might develop a whole new way of curing cancer. Do you have an active child? He could win a gold medal at the Olympics in track. Enjoy the "rosy" side of your children.

What Parents **Really** Do

About twice a year we take out a classified ad in the paper to highlight one of our children's accomplishments. It's usually listed under "miscellaneous" and reads something like:

> Congratulations to Jason Parker.
> At the age of six and a half he is now
> riding his two-wheel bike all by himself.
> Way to go, Jason!

The kids love looking through the paper and reading about themselves.

San Francisco mom with two kids

Keeping Quiet Leads
to Self-Confident Kids

Traditional Parenting Tip

Self-confident children feel secure enough to try new experiences. Children who are constantly told, "Be careful," "Don't touch!" or "Don't do that" begin to doubt their capabilities. Why should they audition for the school play when they aren't talented enough to get a part? The next time your child walks into a room carrying a glass of water, resist the urge to tell him, "Be careful, you're going to spill that."

What Parents **Really** Do

As Sondra began crawling and exploring, our natural inclination was to say "No-no," or "No, that's not yours." Allan suggested, "Why are we saying no? Let's do an experiment and see if we can raise Sondra without saying no." Thus began our experiment. We child proofed the house. If we were at someone else's house and saw her getting into something she shouldn't, we distracted her. Other times we said, "That vase is Susan's. You can touch this book." If she wanted a cookie right before dinner we said, "Yes, you can pick out a cookie now and eat it after your dinner. Do you want to put it on your plate now?" Did we have a wild uncontrollable child? No. (Yikes! I said the "no" word.) By the time she was four, she had two trips to Europe under her belt, and we stayed in bed-and-breakfasts filled with antiques and other valuable items. To this day, people still comment on Sondra's politeness and appropriate behavior.

The "yes" mom, Silvana

Self-Reliant Children

Traditional Parenting Tip

Teaching children self-reliance is a complex task. Watching their faces as they master a new skill makes the hard work pay off. Help children to be successful in one task before encouraging them to move forward again. If your child is learning to ride a two-wheeler, wait a few weeks before bringing out the new roller blades. Self-reliant children use their success in one area to branch out and try something new. We've all heard that "success breeds success." Point out what your child *can* do—like make friends, tie her shoes, or even dress her dolls.

What Parents **Really** Do

When our older daughter Trina was twelve, she frequently did television commercials and modeling. Her concept of "work" meant she earned seventy-five dollars an hour to wear a cute sundress on the runway. In order to give her an awareness of typical wages for preteens, we insisted she spend two weeks every summer picking berries. Each day, at 6:00 A.M., she'd take the dusty berry bus out to the strawberry fields. For eight hours, Trina got hot and dirty, doing manual labor. On a good day, she'd earn ten dollars. It gave her a deep appreciation for the real effort it takes people to earn money.

Silvana

Preparing Pays Off

Traditional Parenting Tip

Mornings can be a rush as everyone races to get ready for school or work. Help your children get in the habit of laying out their clothes and setting their backpacks by the front door each evening, ready for school the next day. That way, no early morning decisions are necessary; just get dressed and grab that backpack. The extra few minutes may even give you time to read your children a short story before the bus comes.

What Parents **Really** Do

My kids dress in sweatpants and T-shirts for school the majority of the time. Since those clothes are comfortable and don't show wrinkles, I decided to let them sleep in their clean school clothes. At night, after their bath, they put on clean underwear and their sweat outfits. The next morning, they simply come downstairs for breakfast, already fully dressed. We find this saves about ten minutes every morning. My kids are in a better mood because there are no clothes hassles to deal with. Now, while they eat breakfast, I read a few headlines from the morning paper and we have an informal lesson on current events.

Theresa Brandwin, teacher

Money Stops Bickering Battles

Traditional Parenting Tip

When children argue and bicker, it is best for parents to stay out of the way. Set ground rules—such as no hitting or bad language—but then let children work out their problems themselves. This teaches them to be responsible for their own behavior. Try not to take sides with children, since they often want you to see their side of the situation and punish their sibling.

What Parents **Really** Do

My three children constantly nitpicked over small things. There was always a squabble over who took the toy from the cereal box or who got to select the cartoon on TV. Now, every Monday, I lay out three rolls of dimes on the kitchen windowsill, labeled with each of their names. The minute anyone starts bickering over a minor incident, I remove a dime from their roll. It's amazing how this has cut down the verbal assaults in our home. Naturally, they get to keep any money in their roll on Sunday nights. The peace is worth the extra money to me.

Quiet-loving mom with three kids

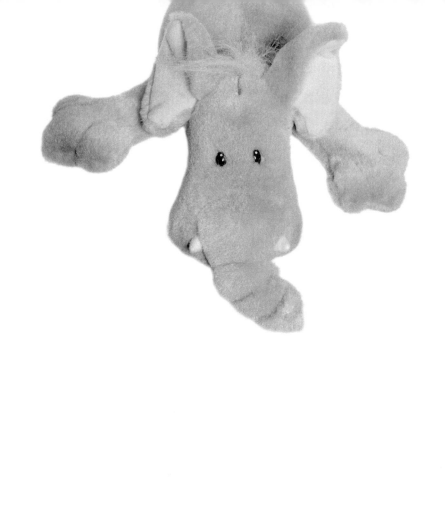

Getting Chores Completed (Even Though They Are Not Quite Up to *House Beautiful* Standards)

Remember when you were a child and had to shovel snow, milk a herd of cows, churn your own butter, and knit your own socks . . . all before breakfast? Kids today don't have any idea about the meaning of chores! Here are some suggestions on how to get your children to give at least a halfhearted attempt at doing their simple chores.

Choose Your Battles

Traditional Parenting Tip

Some parents don't mind messy rooms or dirty dishes in the TV room. Others draw the line at leaving underwear on the bathroom floor. Your children are the first to know what sets off your hot button. (And that's what they'll do anytime they want a reaction from you!) The key to effective parenting is asking yourself objectively, "Why do I get so upset when my daughter leaves her art supplies all over the kitchen table?" If the action is trivial, learn to overlook it. Unless safety is an issue, pretend you are simply visiting your house. How would a guest react if they saw a bowl with caked-on pudding in your son's room?

What Parents **Really** Do

I've found that occasionally embarrassing my child is a quick and efficient way to teach a lesson. Jessica went through a whining stage. All I heard was "Whhyy can't I go to the malllll?" "Do I haaave to walk the dog?" She knew it was the one habit that set me on edge. One day I picked her up after school with two friends. As they got in the car I said, "Pleaasse hurry and buckle up. We need to get going." A few minutes later I added, "Ohhh—traffic is soooo baaaad. I don't think I can staaaand it. Whyyyyy do I always have to be laaaaate?" When Jessica gave me a quizzical look, I simply said, "Wow, Jessica, I think I've picked up your speech patterns." She knew what I meant.

Whining moooom in Wisconsin

Step-by-Step Chores

Traditional Parenting Tip

How often do we give our children a directive and then get upset because the task wasn't up to our standards? Many times children simply don't understand what we want. Instead of frustrating your children, follow these steps:

1. Do the job as they watch. Explain the steps.
2. Have them help you do the job.
3. Let your child do the job as you watch and offer guidance.
4. Get out of the way and let your child do the task alone.

The process is time consuming, but it helps avoid a shouting match of, "But I *did* clean my room!" as you survey piles of clothes, books, and perhaps missing family pets on the floor.

What Parents **<u>Really</u>** Do

Every time my kids tell me I'm mean, I let them know that I've entered the "meanest mom of the year" pageant. Every time they say I'm mean, I get more points toward the crown! They usually respond with, "You could never win; you're not that mean!" I've used this the past three years and still have not won the crown!

Denise Siegel, parks and recreation director

Getting Rid of Clutter

Traditional Parenting Tip

Walk through the average house and you'll find an assortment of misplaced items scattered throughout each room. There's a sock next to the dog's bowl, a stuffed squirrel propped by the toothbrushes, and old homework on top of the TV. Designate ten minutes before bedtime when each child goes through the house, picking up his or her items. Then have an adult make another sweep, collecting overlooked items for the "auction" box. Once a week, auction off the items in the box for twenty-five cents each or in exchange for doing a chore. If a child needs his soccer shin guard, he can pay up or offer to sweep the garage in exchange. Items unclaimed after two weeks are simply discarded or donated. Parents get to keep the money to use for themselves when they go out on one of their sporadic dates.

what Parents **Really** Do

The sack! As a way of getting my younger, somewhat sloppier, daughter to pick up all her clothes, I'd tell her what wasn't off the floor of her bedroom would be put in a sack. Then, as promised, I'd walk into her room with a brown paper bag and promptly place inside whatever was laying on the floor. The contents remained there for a couple days regardless of the inconvenience of having only one shoe in her closet.

Brenda Nixon, author of *Parenting Power in the Early Years*

Consistency and Accountability

Traditional Parenting Tip

I don't understand it," said a frazzled mom. "I tell my kids to pick up the dirty dishes in the TV room, but they ignore me." Children naturally try to challenge authority. The key to discipline is consistency. Do you require that they do homework before talking on the phone? What happens when your daughter insists she has just ten minutes of homework and should be able to call Ashley right now? Unless there's an emergency, stick to your rules. Let children see you hold them accountable to family rules.

What Parents **Really** Do

As a single mother with eight children (five of us teenagers at one time), my mom had a few simple rules. Every child had to maintain a B average, get a part-time job, play one sport or participate in one extracurricular activity, attend church, and be in the house before she locked the door. Mom worked the 3:00 P.M. to 11:00 P.M. shift and stayed up at least an hour or two after getting home. One winter night, my seventeen-year-old brother, Kevin, got home after curfew. He was exhausted and it was too cold to sleep on the porch so he broke into the house. My mother didn't bother explaining the rule but called 911 and had him arrested for breaking and entering. After seeing our brother spend the night in jail, none of us ever broke curfew again.

Carmen Leal, author of *Portraits of Huntington's*

The Power of the Dollar

Traditional Parenting Tip

According to *Zillions* (a magazine for kids by *Consumer Reports*), almost half of American kids get an allowance. Earning and budgeting money is a valuable skill. Think about horror stories you've heard about college students maxing out credit cards. Decide with your child what the allowance will cover. Who will pay for clothing and school lunches? Is an allowance strictly for fun items? Is some money required to be saved? Giving your child some input into handling money increases her ability to make wise financial decisions.

What Parents **Really** Do

Our kids always told us we were tight with our money. On our last vacation, we put them in charge of the entire budget. They had a set amount to spend for our ten-day trip through northern California. The first two days, we lived like kings—fancy hotels, extra desserts for dinner, and even room service. Suddenly, reality hit and they saw the money dwindling fast. They adopted a strict budget. We still had fun, but there were no more trips to the souvenir store. We stayed in cheaper hotels and even had to order only water to drink with our meals. Our kids quickly learned that money doesn't grow on trees.

Money-managing parents

Ring . . . Ring . . . Ring . . .

Traditional Parenting Tip

As parents, our goal is to raise children to be responsible adults. This means teaching children to pick up their clothes, learn basic social skills, and get themselves ready for school in the morning. Make an event of going to the store so your child can select his own alarm clock. Then show him how it works and let him decide what time it should go off each morning. For heavy snoozers, place the clock on the opposite side of the room so they have to get out of bed to turn it off.

What Parents **Really** Do

My ten-year-old daughter is definitely *not* a morning person. She's a heavy sleeper and needs several "prompts" to wake up. Ever since kindergarten, fifteen minutes before she needs to wake up, I slowly rub her back while singing a silly wake-up song. Ten minutes later, I repeat the process. Five minutes before she needs to get up, I sing the song, rub her back, and kiss her neck. For now, I cherish the chance to cuddle her warm body and know I'm helping her start the day feeling loved. She can use an alarm clock in college.

Antialarm clock mom with two kids

Traditional Parenting Tip

Having trouble getting children to do their chores? Set up a rotating job chart. List all the necessary household duties that need to be done, ranging from cleaning toilets to walking the dog. (If children have a wide age range, color code the jobs suitable for preschoolers.) On a designated day each week, select job assignments. Some families state that every person must select three jobs. Knowing that all family members have chores to do solves the problem of, "Why do I have to take out the trash?" Plus, it's a nice feeling to know you only have to clean the cat litter box for a week before the job is reassigned.

What Parents **Really** Do

I worked for six years as a resident director in a boarding school program for high school students. There were eight students in the house and four staff members, who were mostly all college students themselves. As you can imagine, keeping the house clean was nearly impossible! Each week the kids had their own chores that they were required to do on a daily basis (wash dishes, take out trash, straighten up a room in the house). Each week we designated one student to be the House Diva (all the students were young women); her chore for the week was to enforce that everyone else did their chores. Though this person literally had no real work to do, this was perhaps the most hated chore. "Such and such never does her chore," the House Diva would say. "I can't stand this job—nobody listens to me," she would cry. The other resident director and I knew exactly how she felt. This designation not only helped the students to understand the difficulties of our role as resident directors, but it also motivated them to do their chores when they weren't the House Diva to make things easier on whoever was. It worked out brilliantly and our house has been much tidier!

Michelle Rief

89

The Power of Natural Consequences

Traditional Parenting Tip

At one time or another, parents (usually moms) get tired of being unappreciated when it comes to household chores. Of course, everyone is expected to chip in and help, but Mom usually ends up doing the majority of work. Let natural consequences take place. If Junior hasn't turned on the dishwasher, sit down at the dinner table and calmly say, "All the silverware is still dirty. Junior, what should we do?" Is your daughter's soccer uniform dirty because she forgot to put it in the hamper? I guess she'll go to the game with a muddy shirt. Instead of nagging, let natural consequences teach the lesson. The key is to display your dramatic abilities by remaining a calm, collected adult. Don't get in an argument with your children. Smile sweetly and in an innocent voice say, "I certainly can't drive to the mall in a filthy car. Amber, let me know when you've completed your chore of cleaning the car so I can drive you."

What Parents **Really** Do

You've seen the fictionalized stories about parents going on strike on TV. In our house, we turned fiction into reality. My wife and I were fed up with our children taking us for granted. One Saturday morning we literally went on strike. I even used a computer program to print us T-shirts that said, "We're on strike until we get some respect!" We marched through their bedrooms chanting silly phrases and made-up slogans. Then, the entire weekend, we did nothing but read, putter around the house, and relax. No cooking, no driving, no reading stories. We were on strike!

I loved hearing our oldest son calling a friend's mom for a ride to a soccer game and having to explain that his parents were on strike. By Sunday night, they promised to redeem their ways if only we'd return to "normal." We made them grovel a few more hours until we called off the strike. We're saving the T-shirts, though, just in case!

Protesting mom and dad

Cleaning Contract

Traditional Parenting Tip

Different parents have different tolerance levels for messy rooms. Some parents are enthusiastic if they see a patch of carpet under the clothes on the floor. Others feel children's clothes need to be neatly folded in drawers, and toys arranged alphabetically on shelves. Work out a compromise with your children. Even though it is "their" room, you do buy almost everything they own and let them keep it in a house you pay for. You have the right to set cleanliness standards. Write down the specifics of an acceptable level of "mess." Perhaps that means books can be scattered on the desk and up to four items of clothing on the floor. Set a clear standard and have children work to meet it.

What Parents **Really** Do

We set up an indoor basketball hoop over our son's laundry basket. Now he enjoys wadding up dirty laundry and shooting it from across the room. He gives himself three points if the dirty laundry hits the hamper as he stands in the door-way across the room.

Teacher and mom

Buying Peace and Quiet

Traditional Parenting Tip

Allowances are a tool to teach children how to handle money. Provide children with a weekly amount of money with the stipulation that they set some aside for long-term savings (perhaps for a new bike or video game), some for tithing or charity, and some to spend right away as they please. If they want to earn extra money, post additional chores they can do, along with the amount you'll pay. Then it's up to them if they want to rake leaves or vacuum the car to help reach their financial goals.

What Parents **Really** Do

I know children should have to do actual "work" to earn money. There are times, however, when I use money to buy some peace and quiet. I've told my children I'd pay them one dollar each if they are quiet during a twenty-minute call to my best friend. Sometimes they get paid so I can take an undisturbed nap on a Sunday afternoon. I've even paid them just to leave me alone and not bang on the bathroom door when I want to take a bubble bath. It's cheaper than therapy!

Samantha Trillium, customer service representative

The Case of the Missing Toys

Traditional Parenting Tip

Picking up toys should be a child's responsibility. Preschoolers need help, of course, in learning how to put things away correctly. By the time children reach elementary school, they should be able to return puzzle pieces to the box, put books on bookshelves, and return toys to storage spaces. Help your children by labeling shelves and cupboards so they can easily identify where each item goes. Reduce clutter by occasionally working together to discard broken or unused toys.

What Parents **Really** Do

My kids left their toys all over the house, ignoring my pleas to pick them up. One particularly messy Sunday afternoon, I heard myself yelling, "If you don't pick up these toys, I'm throwing them out!" My children ignored me. The next morning after they left for school, I made good on my threat. (Partially!) Gathering several large boxes, I went through the house and collected ALL their toys. This included books, CDs, favorite stuffed animals, Legos, you name it. Then I took the boxes to a neighbor's for storage so my kids couldn't find the toys. It was worth the extra work just to see their faces when they came home to a toyless house. We sat down and I calmly told them I was tired of nagging them to pick up toys. Now there would be no more nagging, because there were no more toys. They complained and moaned and groaned, but it was three weeks before I relented and let them have four toys each. I gradually returned all their toys and let them know if things were not picked up, everything would disappear once again.

Mother of five children

Part 4

Creating Family Traditions (Howl at the Moon and Collect Souvenir Rocks)

In thinking back to your own childhood, you probably remember cherished traditions like eating Sunday dinner at Grandma's and always getting new shoes for Easter. Discover ways to create lasting traditions with your own family.

Summertime Learning

Traditional Parenting Tip

Parents would turn cartwheels to be able to have a three-month summer vacation with little required of them. Children, on the other hand, have a tendency to utter that all-too-frequent phrase, "There's nothing to do." Since children are used to school assignments, give them summertime assignments also. Require at least fifteen minutes of reading every day. Help them start a new hobby or a sticker collection. You don't need to assign hours of schoolwork, simply a few activities to keep their creative juices going. Try planting a family garden or building a playhouse. One mother required that her children do one brief worksheet of basic multiplication or division every day. They returned to school with a firm grasp of basic math.

What Parents **Really** Do

Every summer I assign a project for Sondra to do. One summer she was to work on a scrapbook depicting her summer activities. She took pictures and we bought fancy paper. As she created colorful pages of photos, she wrote detailed descriptions. We now have a comprehensive photo scrapbook of the summer of 2000. Plenty of time remained to swim and relax, but the activity gave her a semistructured focus to the summer. The next year her assignment was to complete the Tiger Woods program cosponsored by Target stores. She actually won a $2,500 scholarship!

If you're interested in this program, look up www.startsomething.target.com.

Silvana

Find the Sunny Side of Every Situation

Traditional Parenting Tip

Astudy of strong, happy families by the University of Nebraska interviewed over seventeen thousand people from twenty-seven countries. The research showed these "model" families had a ratio of ten to one for positive to negative interactions. In some cases, there were twenty positive interactions to every one negative comment. Look for ways to find the silver lining in what normally could be a dark cloud.

What Parents **Really** Do

My son studied violin for three years and had natural talent. His teacher agreed that Dylan was gifted. As my son entered middle school, he begged to stop the lessons. "I don't like to play," he repeated over and over. "I want to join the wrestling team." "What?" I thought. My son with the talented fingers wants to go flop on a mat with sweaty boys bigger than him? Were we teaching him to be a quitter? We decided he wasn't quitting violin. He was moving on—graduating. We planned his violin farewell concert by inviting friends and relatives over. He played a few of his favorite pieces (to a standing ovation of course), and then we served cake and ice cream. Several months later Dylan developed a self-motivated interest in computers, and he just designed his first web site.

Home schooling mom with four children

Forget Keeping Up with the Joneses

Traditional Parenting Tip

Keeping up with the Joneses only leads to frustration. Establish the values you think are important for your family. Would you rather spend money to go skiing on weekends as a family, or add a hot tub to the backyard? Take pride in establishing your own traditions and lifestyle. You'll be setting an example for your children to look for ways to live a creative life without worrying about other people's opinions.

What Parents **Really** Do

Our family likes taking short weekend trips to various festivals and tourist attractions. Being on a limited budget, we bring picnic lunches and camp if possible. To avoid expensive purchases at souvenir shops, we began a tradition of finding "the most special rock" on each trip. The whole family has to agree on one rock to take home. Each rock is then labeled and placed on a sturdy shelf in the living room as a reminder of our family time together. Neighborhood kids actually come over to look at our rock collection. We certainly never have to worry about these treasures breaking! Our children think souvenir shops are only for "looking."

Rock-collecting mom and administrative assistant

Gifts from the Heart

Traditional Parenting Tip

It's all too easy to run into a store and buy your child a new toy or video game . . . even when it's not a special occasion. Instead of spending money, try spending time with your child and giving "gifts from the heart." These gifts can be as simple as saying "please" and "thank you" to your child in ordinary conversations. Make a list of all your child's positive characteristics and put it on the refrigerator. Work on a volunteer project together, like collecting canned goods from the neighbors. Ask your child to tell about a movie he saw and really listen to all the inconsequential details. Let your child know the excitement you felt on the day of her birth. Gifts from the heart can never be purchased with money.

What Parents **Really** Do

My mom was celebrating her seventy-fifth birthday and certainly didn't need any more wind chimes, scented candles, or slippers. I really agonized over what to give her. Finally inspiration hit. My son helped me decoupage a simple box with colorful pictures of our family, including relatives. Then came the hard part. My husband, son, and I took a stack of fifty-two 3" x 5" index cards and wrote something positive about my mom. Some were simple statements like "Grandma, I love how you let me watch cartoons when I visit you." I wrote down memories I had of her helping me sew a new dress for the prom, and how we would ice-skate on our pond. At her birthday party, she was instructed to read one card every Monday morning to start her week out on a positive note. My son saw how happy it made his grandma and said, "Mom, that was a great present. I hope someday someone gives me one like that." Naturally I'm busy filling out index cards for his birthday next month!

Cheap but creative mom

Appreciate the Little Things

Traditional Parenting Tip

Television tells us all that we need "The newest! The largest! The best!" No wonder children have difficulty learning to be appreciative for what they have. Try to foster an attitude of thankfulness in your children. Thank your spouse for driving all of you to church. Leave a "Thank you for brushing the dog" note on your child's pillow. Point out how the rain glistens on the leaves as the sun comes out. At dinner, discuss all the good things that happened during the day.

What Parents Really Do

Something I do to teach my boys the importance of starting their day off right with the Lord is a practice I learned from Ephesians 6:13–18, about putting on the armor of God. Each day as I drive my boys, ages nine and six, to school, we mimic "putting on" each of the six pieces of armor, stating them aloud: "We put on the helmet of salvation, the breastplate of righteousness, the belt of truth, the shoes of peace, the shield of faith, and the sword of the Spirit." Then we pray for God to bless our day and to protect and guide each of us. We have been doing this for more than two years, and it only takes a couple of minutes each morning. The boys love this and even take turns leading in praying!

Laura Sabin Riley, author of *All Mothers Are Working Mothers* and *The ABC's of Character*

Traditional Parenting Tip

When our children are little, it seems so natural to cuddle them on our lap and read to them frequently. As they begin reading on their own, it's easy to assume they are too big for read-aloud time. As children get older, continue reading out loud, whether it's a devotional book or the daily newspaper. If you have slow eaters, read a book while they finish eating. Instead of nagging them to "hurry up and eat," end mealtime on a positive note by getting everyone involved in the story. Pretend you're on the radio and read with distinctive voices. Come on—there's a bit of "ham" in all of us!

What Parents **Really** Do

One of our nieces is big into Lambchops. Anything with a lamb or sheep she has to have. She even dragged home a baby crib that had a lamb painted on it that she found along the curb! Anyway, I've read the Christmas story from the Gospel of Luke to her and personalized it to: "There were lambchop keepers keeping watch over their lambchops by night," and "The Lord is my Lambchop Keeper." And to her, gyros are lambchop sandwiches!

John L. Hoh Jr.

The Art of Empathy

Traditional Parenting Tip

Children have a tendency to see the world only from their point of view. Teach empathy skills by asking questions like, "What do you think that homeless man is thinking as he sits on the bench?" "Why did Grandma get teary eyed when she read your poem?" Get them thinking about what you or your spouse does during the day. Encourage times of conversation when everyone gives his or her opinions on a certain topic. Children need to learn to be aware of a world beyond their personal lives.

What Parents **Really** Do

I work out of my home. This means my kids take it for granted that I get them ready for school in the morning and greet them in the afternoon. In fact, they took it for granted a few too many times. After being unappreciated for too long, I announced, "Next week, we're pretending I have a traditional job. I'll need to get to 'work' earlier than you go to school. I've arranged for before- and after-school care through the YMCA. I'll drop you off at the Y an hour earlier than you usually get up. They'll take you to school. After school, the Y bus will take you back to the center. I'll pick you up at 5:30." Their shocked faces were priceless! Amid many complaints, they spent a week at the YMCA learning to appreciate the benefits of having a stay-at-home mom.

"Domestic engineer" with three kids

Traditional Parenting Tip

We all have good intentions about teaching our children to help others less fortunate. Yet somehow we never get around to serving soup at a soup kitchen or mowing an elderly neighbor's lawn. Look for those "teachable moments" that give children an awareness of ways they can help. When driving through McDonald's, order an extra burger and milk to give to a homeless person on the corner. Save the unused bottles of shampoo and soap from hotels to give to the homeless. Next time you have a family get-together, ask everyone to bring a can of food. Take your children with you as you deliver the cans to a local food bank.

What Parents **Really** Do

We always buy a season pass to the local children's museum. One benefit of membership is getting four free guest passes. Instead of using the passes for friends, we donate them to a local shelter for battered women. The museum visit is a special treat for women and children who normally wouldn't get to go to the museum.

Mom and photographer

The Security of Routines

Traditional Parenting Tip

Children respond favorably to routines. Knowing that bedtime consists of a bath, two stories, a song, and then bedtime prayers helps children settle down for the evening. In the same way, setting routines for chores or doing homework helps children know what is expected. There's a reassurance in knowing Dad always wrestles with the kids when he comes home. Children gain the security of being in a stable home by knowing daily routines.

what Parents **Really** Do

Sondra and I have a quiet morning routine. While she eats a healthy breakfast, I, the ever-dutiful mother, read to her from a devotional book or the newspaper. There's no TV or radio in the background, so she starts the day with a calm atmosphere. One morning, as she ate crepes and I read an article from *Newsweek,* my husband burst in the door. "Sondra!" he yelled. "I have ten minutes to challenge you to a tetherball game!" She raced outside in her pajamas and had an exhilarating time of tetherball in the cool morning with her fun-loving dad. I continued reading *Newsweek* in peace.

Silvana

Going to the Dogs

Traditional Parenting Tip

Teaching children the importance of compassion is a long-term goal for parents. We tell them Jesus wants us to be kind, yet we sometimes forget to demonstrate that concept in a practical manner. Look for ways to teach compassion on a regular basis.

- Set out bird food on a winter day.
- Draw a picture and write a letter to an elderly relative.
- Donate good quality toys to a shelter for abused children.
- Volunteer to weed the yard at church and plant colorful flowers.
- Greet people who move into your neighborhood.

What Parents **Really** Do

Yes, my heart goes out to homeless people who are asking for food or money. Sometimes a scruffy-looking dog accompanies them. Being a dog lover myself, I began carrying small bags of dog food or dog biscuits in my car. When I see homeless people with dogs, I give them the dog food and tell them I understand the importance of a dog's companionship. My family thinks I'm crazy, but I feel good helping hungry dogs.

Dog-loving mom

Storing Creative Masterpieces

Traditional Parenting Tip

Watercolors of flowers blooming in the garden. Papier-mâché dinosaurs. Modern art vases made out of clay. No, these aren't displays at a world-class museum. They're simply the artwork brought home from school on a regular basis. So what do you do with the creations your budding Picasso brings home? When the refrigerator is covered, string a clothesline along the hallway and attach drawings by clothespins. Use larger pieces as wrapping paper. Select favorite pictures to laminate and use as placemats. Still too much artwork? Package it up and send to doting grandparents!

What Parents **Really** Do

With three young children, I was overwhelmed with an abundance of artwork. Much of it on *large* pieces of paper! After trying various solutions, we've come up with the "Friday Afternoon Art Show." Each child selects that week's favorite piece of artwork, which gets proudly displayed on the garage ceiling. Yes, I need a ladder and my back gets sore from bending over backwards to attach the pictures to the ceiling, but my house is no longer covered with finger paintings and life-sized paper body tracings.

Mom with a kink in her back

Hurray for the Tooth Fairy!

Traditional Parenting Tip

L et's face it. Even though we strive as parents to be honest and truthful with our children, there comes a time when we announce the arrival of the tooth fairy. "Just put your bloody little baby tooth under your pillow and the tooth fairy will get it tonight," we tell our gap-toothed first-grader. Then we wonder if we're destroying our child's psyche by "lying" to them. The majority of psychologists tell us not to worry. Harmless, fun aspects of childhood such as looking for eggs left by the Easter bunny or finding a quarter left by the tooth fairy will not turn our children into therapy-seeking adults.

What Parents **Really** Do

I'd been trying to get our two-year-old to get rid of his beloved pacifier, but nothing worked. Our six-year-old came home from school, ecstatic about losing her first tooth. I explained, in great detail (with the two-year-old listening), how the tooth fairy worked. The next morning, both kids were amazed to see that the tooth was gone, and in its place, under the pillow, was a handheld Etch-a-Sketch. I told my son the "pacifier fairy" would leave him a toy under his pillow in exchange for his pacifier. Sure enough, the next morning, the pacifier was gone, replaced by a new toy car.

Mom, a.k.a. "pacifier fairy"

Traditional Parenting Tip

Christmas is a perfect time to create long-lasting family traditions. Make a list with your family of the traditions they enjoy most. You'll be surprised how some family members place great importance on events you find inconsequential. A child might tell how her favorite tradition is filling the bird feeder on Christmas Eve so the birds can enjoy a holiday feast. Add to the list each year as a way of keeping track of family memories.

What Parents **Really** Do

As the mother of three girls under the age of six, I felt our family didn't have any "real" traditions. Everywhere I went, from Sunday school to MOPS meetings, people talked about their wonderful, creative traditions. I decided to be the perfect mother, creating memories galore. Our house became a whirlwind of disjointed activities as we baked cookies, designed our own wrapping paper, sang carols at bedtime, read the story of Jesus' birth nightly, and attended every community festival or celebration I could find. All the while, I kept telling my family, "This will be our holiday tradition!" We all ended up tired and cranky. Now our tradition is kidding Mom about the year she tried to set a world record for creating the most traditions in a single holiday season!

Angela Sing, mother of three girls

Traditional Parenting Tip

Children benefit from having traditions and family rituals. There's a sense of security in knowing that on Sunday mornings everyone cuddles together on the couch to read the comics. Children enjoy knowing they get to select the meal for their birthday dinner. If you have few family traditions, start developing some now. How about always serving green mashed potatoes on St. Patrick's Day? Or serving root beer floats on report card days?

What Parents **Really** Do

I know many families have very "traditional traditions" like serving Grandma's special cranberry salad each Thanksgiving. Our family is a little on the unconventional side, so we create traditions that are a bit off-the-wall. Whenever there's a full moon, we go outside and howl like wolves. (The neighbors are used to it!) When someone has a birthday, all the family members wake up the birthday person by forming a marching band. We use pots and pans for instruments and march around the bedroom. Our kids have developed a real sense of humor by seeing that it's okay to have fun on a regular basis as a family.

Wolf-howling mom with four kids

Dealing with the Mundane Aspects of Life (Bedtime, Meals, Shopping, Cleaning the Lint Trap)

Wouldn't it be wonderful to have a life filled with servants, exotic vacations, and a country home in Switzerland? Until we win the lottery, most of us are destined to have a life that includes cleaning the lint trap. Here are some ways to add "color" to ordinary routines.

Car Kid of the Day

Traditional Parenting Tip

Why is it children get in a car and immediately begin their plaintive wails of "Mom, Jordan's looking at me"? Then there's the struggle over who sits in which seat and who gets to decide which fast-food place to visit after soccer practice. Solve the backseat bickering by purchasing a small calendar. On an alternating basis, write a child's name on each date and keep the calendar in the car. Now, each day as you get in, check the calendar to find out who is "Car Kid of the Day." That child selects where he'll sit, which radio station to listen to, and whatever else needs deciding. Since everyone knows his or her turn is coming up, there is less complaining.

What Parents **Really** Do

When my children bicker in the car, I tell them I'm going to sell them to the gypsies. They never believed me until one day we drove past a sign saying "Gypsonville" and I told them that is where the gypsies live. Now they're worried enough to keep quiet!

Shelley Petrowski, recreation director

Overcoming the Dark

Traditional Parenting Tip

Many children develop a fear of the dark. Since this is a normal developmental process, parents simply need to provide their children with reassurance. A set bedtime routine, along with a simple prayer, provides a feeling of security. Make a special occasion out of going to the store and selecting their own nightlight. Some children need a bedside lamp with a dim setting. Ask your child if she prefers a nightlight or a lamp. Having control over the situation often eases the fear.

What Parents **Really** Do

I decorated a plastic spray bottle with sequins and glitter. It's quite exquisite. I filled the bottle with water and added a few drops of blue food coloring. Then I added a few drops of peppermint extract. This is now my "Antimonster Spray." Before my son goes to sleep, he sprays under his bed, in his closet, and by the windows with this magical potion that keeps all monsters away from our house.

Mother and court reporter

Stuffed Animals on the Ceiling Fan

Traditional Parenting Tip

Bedtime often becomes a power struggle as kids ask for one more story, another glass of water, and a longer back rub. Beat the bedtime blues by establishing a consistent schedule. Have your children help you list the six or seven steps that happen before being tucked into bed. For younger children, make a chart using magazine pictures so they can identify the process. They can glance at the chart and know the steps:

- Brush teeth
- Put on pajamas
- Get in bed
- Parent reads two stories
- Parent and child sing a song together
- Kisses and hugs
- Lights out!

What Parents **Really** Do

We finally found a bedroom routine that has worked for the last six months. (I'm hoping it works until they leave for college!) The boys share a room and each has a favorite stuffed animal he sleeps with. While they brush their teeth, I hide or disguise the animals somewhere in the room. After putting on their pajamas, my two boys, ages six and eight, go into the bathroom to brush their teeth. Part of the fun is closing the bathroom door completely so I can do my "job." One night might find a teddy bear wearing sunglasses and a baseball cap at the back of the closet. Another time "Mike the Monkey" is hiding in the underwear drawer. I admit I actually spend time at work thinking where I can hide those silly stuffed animals. I've even resorted to tying each one by the leg and hanging them from the ceiling fan. (The animals, not my sons!) My boys come out of the bathroom, find their stuffed animals, listen to a story, and go to bed. The rule is: If you get out of bed, your stuffed animal doesn't get to participate in the next night's frivolity!

Part-time stuffed animal wrangler

Get Well Soon

Traditional Parenting Tip

No one likes being sick. Children have an especially hard time understanding why they feel bad and need to rest in bed. The following are three ways to take some of the misery from your little one's illness:

1. If your children have the chicken pox or other itchy spots, let them use cotton swabs to dab calamine lotion on their bodies. This turns their entire body into a giant dot-to-dot.
2. Keep a "Get Well Soon" kit to be used only when children need to stay in bed. Fill a plastic container with modeling clay, stickers, and a box of new markers. This special-treat box helps pass the time as they read new books or make a craft.
3. Set up your child's sickroom like a hotel. He or she can order room service (you provide the food) or get your attention by ringing a special bell.

What Parents **Really** Do

When my son had the chicken pox, I told him if he scratched, he would grow feathers—that's where the name came from!

Valerie Allen

Messy Mixtures and Conversation

Traditional Parenting Tip

Cooking with your children is a great way to share information and conversation. Your normally shy child just might open up to you about a problem at school as you're both kneading bread dough. For a great recipe that you'll never want to eat, mix up a batch of Goop.

Goop the Great

Mix 1 cup *cold* water and 1 cup Elmer's glue (must use Elmer's) and stir. In a separate bowl, mix 1 tablespoon Boraxo with 1/2 cup very hot water (not boiling). You can add a few drops of food coloring to the water and Boraxo mixture. Add the hot water mixture slowly to the glue and water. Mix a few seconds and suddenly the Goop forms! Keeps covered in the refrigerator for weeks.

This substance is great to stretch and feel oozing through your fingers.

What Parents **Really** Do

I'm the youngest of six children, and we were all very close in age. My mother liked to bake our famous family recipe for molasses cookies. And, of course, all six of us wanted to lick the spoon with the leftover molasses on it. One day, we were acting like kids do and fighting over who was getting the spoon. My mother decided to solve the problem right then. She poured a cup of molasses into Tupperware bowls for each of us and we had to eat it. Needless to say, molasses cookie spoons never quite had the same appeal for all of us!

Carmen Leal, author of *Portraits of Huntington's*

Not Hungry? Don't Eat!

Traditional Parenting Tip

American parents often worry that their children aren't eating properly. It becomes a fight to get children to eat healthy fruits and vegetables. Relax. Study after study shows children *do* get the nutrients they need. All too often, eating is simply a power struggle! No matter how hard you try and how many bribes you make, you can't force your child to eat. The less important you make it seem, the less important it becomes to your child. Don't call your child a finicky eater. Supply healthy foods (which means cleaning out the snack cupboard) and step back. If they don't want dinner, remove their plate and say cheerfully, "That's fine if you don't want meat loaf. You can eat something else tomorrow at breakfast."

what Parents **Really** Do

My first-grader is oh-so-picky about food. He hates any type of vegetable. He does, however, like pancakes. Every morning, little does he know I always mix in a jar of strained baby food zucchini or squash in his pancake batter.

Tricky mom

"Flap and Wiggle" Game

Traditional Parenting Tip

Parents of young children know that ordinary experiences like going to a restaurant can cause children to act inappropriately. Plan accordingly and be prepared. Avoid going to restaurants during peak times when waiting time is long. Ask to see a menu when you first arrive. Then you can give the server your order right away. After you order, take a leisurely trip to the rest room to wash hands, passing more time until the food arrives at your table.

What Parents **Really** Do

While waiting for our food to arrive at a restaurant, we play "Flap and Wiggle Hide-and-Seek." The person who is "it" gets to hide a small object while another family member closes his eyes. She might hide a sugar packet under the breadbasket or stick it in the dried flower arrangement. The player opens his eyes and, using his fingers, "walks" around the table, searching for the hidden item. The rest of the family hold their napkins—giving nonverbal cues. The closer the walking fingers get to the item, the more furiously the family members wiggle their napkins, similar to the "hot-cold" game. Ignore the stares of people around you who wonder why they are sitting next to a table of laughing people waving napkins.

Fun-loving stay-at-home mom

Rice for the Weekend

Traditional Parenting Tip

Picky eaters cause parents literally to dance around the kitchen to get their child to eat wholesome foods. The options are many:

- Ask their "opinion" about a new dish. They'll taste it to be able to report back to other family members.
- Insist they try one bite of a new food.
- Don't make a big deal out of it. If she wants to eat only cereal for a solid week, let her.
- Try changing the texture of the food, such as raw broccoli instead of cooked.
- Have children help prepare the meal. They are more likely to eat if they have a part in the preparation.

What Parents **Really** Do

I was fed up with my eight-year-old and ten-year-old constantly picking at their food and demanding special meals. So one Friday afternoon I cleaned out the refrigerator of all leftovers and froze whatever I could. I also packed up all the cookies and treats from the snack cupboard. When my children came home from school, I calmly explained that this weekend we were going to eat like people in Third World countries ate. Their eyes widened in shock as I explained there would be no snacks and only rice and water for dinner. Saturday morning breakfast consisted of complaints and more rice. By lunch, my kids were cranky, but I hung in there and served rice. Dinner was a treat with rice and one apple, shared among the four of us. Sunday breakfast consisted of one piece of dry toast and a tiny glass of milk each. At noon, my kids were very hungry. While eating their bowl of plain rice, I explained how tired I was of them being picky eaters. From now on, they had a choice of eating what I served, or they could have a bowl of rice. It worked. We had very few complaints from then on.

Sharon Lillet   145

Traditional Parenting Tip

No one likes to get shots, especially children. The problem is compounded when parents convey their own anxiety to their children. How often have we said, "Don't worry, Melissa, the shot won't hurt at all"? Then the nurse sticks a needle in the child's arm and it *does* hurt. Prepare young children ahead of time for a doctor's visit. Ask them to remember what they saw in the doctor's office at the last visit. Were there toys? Was there a new fish in the aquarium? What was the doctor wearing? If your child is scheduled for an immunization, explain that the shot will hurt for a brief time. Ask the nurse to have your child blow a big "puff" of air as the shot is given.

What Parents **Really** Do

My twenty-year-old remembers (I certainly do not) when she was a tot that I sat in the pediatrician's office with her insisting she get immunizations. Through her resistance, I finally told her if she didn't get her shots her tongue would turn green and fall out! She got the shot and her immunizations are still up-to-date.

Brenda Nixon, author of *Parenting Power in the Early Years*

Singing Away Bad Behavior

Traditional Parenting Tip

By the time children reach elementary school, they know the basics of proper behavior: no name-calling, use manners, respect adults, don't poke your little brother in the eye, don't tell Grandpa his breath stinks. In most cases gentle, consistent reminders help children remember what they've been taught. Try weaving rules of behavior into everyday conversation. When discussing an upcoming long drive to cousin Ted's house, ask, "What are some things you and your brother can do to help pass time in the car as we drive?" Tell stories about a situation that happened to you in which someone displayed polite behavior. Periodic conversations are more effective than saying all at once: "Here's five things you better do when we get to the play or you're in big trouble!"

What Parents **Really** Do

We were taking the city bus to the library. My eight-year-old and ten-year-old began poking and bothering each other. Instead of lecturing, I stood up and announced to everyone sitting around us, "It seems my children need to have a more positive outlook on life. Will you all join me in singing to them? Let's begin with 'You Are My Sunshine.'" I started singing and so did most of the startled bus passengers. My kids were so mortified. They hardly made eye contact with me for three days. Next time we rode the bus, they were on their best behavior.

Singing Dad

Traditional Parenting Tip

I f children are left home alone, have plenty of snacks on hand that don't require cooking, and make sure they understand basic safety rules. Instead of telling a phone caller, "My dad's not home right now," they can say, "My dad can't come to the phone just now. Can I have your number so he can call you back?" Post important phone numbers to Grandma, neighbors, and poison control by *each* phone.

What Parents **Really** Do

To teach my children to take phone messages, once a week I call them after school, disguising my voice. (Though I suspect they know who I am.) "Hello," I say in a squeaky voice. "This message is for Samantha's dad. Please tell him the pet elephant he bought for Samantha can be picked up. He'll need to bring a two-ton truck and three bales of hay. Call me at 734-1212." When I get home, I check if the kids wrote down the correct information. It's great practice for taking down "real" messages.

Dad and carpenter

151

Traditional Parenting Tip

When children want a major item such as a new mountain bike or top-of-the-line skateboard, help them earn the money. Have a brainstorming session listing ways they could save the amount they need. (Don't forget to include a story about how you slaved for a new Schwinn bike by shoveling snow for thirty-five cents an hour.) Bring home a book from the library listing ways kids earn money. Can they be helpers for children's birthday parties? Can they walk the neighbor's dogs? How about earning money putting up and taking down neighborhood garage sale signs? Children appreciate items more if they help earn the money to buy them.

What Parents Really Do

"Are you absolutely sure you want a horse?" my husband asked our daughter. Like all twelve-year-old girls, she answered with an enthusiastic, "Of course!" "Follow me," directed Allan. They soon returned from the garage, carrying an assortment of boards, nails, and even a ladder. Thirty minutes later, when the pounding and sawing ended, Sondra had a wooden horse fourteen and a half hands high in her room. The "head" end was nailed to her window with a ladder supporting it. Pillows made up for a saddle. She proudly sat on her life-sized horse and stopped bugging us for a real horse. (Well, at least for a few weeks.)

Silvana

Red Towel Saves the Day

Traditional Parenting Tip

Just when you think the house is totally child-proofed for your crawling baby, she learns to walk and discovers all sorts of new safety hazards. Then, as preschoolers, children face hazards with playgroups or at the playground. Since we can't raise our children in a foam-protected world, other safety factors need to be considered. Check your child's slide on summer days. The hot plastic can hurt bare skin. Keep stairs free from books and other items to prevent tripping. Remove long drawstrings from your child's hooded sweatshirts; these can get caught on playground equipment.

What Parents **Really** Do

One day I saw a bright red towel on sale. It didn't particularly match my pale yellow color scheme in the bathroom, but I bought it anyway. After cutting it up into washcloth-sized pieces, I wet each piece and stuck them in the freezer. Now, when one of my four children cuts a lip or scrapes a knee, I bring out the red towel ice packs. The blood doesn't show up as I try to clean their wounds. Nothing's worse than having your three-year-old see a white washcloth covered with her blood.

Mom and former nurse

Blame It on the Dog

Traditional Parenting Tip

Potty training is one of those parenting milestones we all experience. As parents, we want nothing more than to see our little one wear "big kid underwear" and use the toilet unassisted. To make potty training easier, try these tips: Make sure your child is ready to transition out of diapers. Can he pull his pants up and down? Is she interested in watching other people use the toilet? Does he let you know his diaper is wet or dirty? Does she say words for urine or bowel movements? Give children the chance to flush the toilet after an adult uses it. Yes, it's embarrassing to you, but simply another learning tool for your toddler.

What Parents **Really** Do

My two-and-a-half-year-old loves to be naked. She gets in the house and immediately takes off all her clothes. One day, desperate to keep her dressed, I told her at least put her pants on because the dog gets embarrassed if she is naked. That worked so well we now get her to stop crying by saying it upsets the dog. Basically, we blame the dog for everything.

Hy Schwartz, development director, S&S Crafts Worldwide

Avoid Threats Made under Duress!

Traditional Parenting Tip

If you don't get your homework done right now, you're grounded for a year!" Most parents make outlandish threats in the heat of frustration. Then they need to backpedal in order to justify the threat. If your child is not obeying, try alternatives to threats. "I'm going to sit here with you and read your homework assignment to you" is more effective than a one-year grounding. When you do need to dole out punishment, wait until you're in a calmer mood. "I'm going to think about how long you're grounded. In an hour we'll sit down and discuss the situation." If you are calm, your decision-making process will be rational and you won't have to apologize for threatening to send your child to a boarding school in Siberia.

What Parents **Really** Do

I threatened to call Santa if my children did some particular thing. Then I'd pick up the phone, announce that I was calling Santa, and begin dialing. It was an effective behavior modifier.

Lauren Vaughn

Acting Appropriately

Traditional Parenting Tip

B e a good boy," we might tell our son. "I hope you're not bad at the museum," we might say to our daughter. Instead of labeling a child "bad" or "good," try discussing "inappropriate" or "appropriate" behavior. Children can understand that running and yelling is totally appropriate at the park but inappropriate at the library. Ask them to describe appropriate behavior when going to a live theater performance. Children may not know that theater is different from watching a video at home. It's inappropriate to chatter nonstop with the person next to you while actors are performing. An additional plus: children like "big" words such as appropriate and inappropriate.

What Parents **Really** Do

My husband and I role-play appropriate and inappropriate behavior on a regular basis. It's easy to tell your seven-year-old, "Behave yourself on the airplane trip," but what does that mean? I'll say to my husband, "Jeff, please show us the inappropriate way to act on an airplane." Jeff earns an Academy Award, kicking the seat, pushing the flight attendant's call button, throwing down books, and yelling out, "I want off this plane!" Then he models the perfect child, displaying "appropriate" behavior. Our kids love watching his outlandish antics, yet they also get to see what appropriate behavior looks like.

Parents who wish they were on Broadway

Setting Pint-Sized Goals

Traditional Parenting Tip

When your child is involved with a major school assignment or other special event, help her set realistic goals. Is the report on Texas due in two weeks? Help your child make a daily schedule of what she needs to do to complete the project by the due date. Provide gentle reminders to check the list so she can stay on task, but avoid doing the job for her.

What Parents **Really** Do

My daughter had her heart set on getting the lead in the church musical. Ten days before the audition, she received a lengthy monologue in the mail to memorize. I helped her break it down into sections, suggesting she memorize four lines every day. This gave plenty of time to learn the part with confidence. Naturally, she procrastinated. I knew several other girls were hard at work memorizing their lines, so it was hard to keep quiet and not nag her. The night before the audition, she was in tears because she barely knew the lines. My temptation was to say, "I told you so." Instead, I kept quiet, busily cleaning out my office. Naturally, she bombed at the audition. A few months later, when auditions rolled around for the Christmas musical, she practiced ahead of time and actually got the lead!

Irene Gunnersen

Open Conversation with Open Questions

Traditional Parenting Tip

When asking children about their day, use open-ended sentences. This results in a higher chance for intelligent conversation. If you ask your child a closed question such as, "Did you have a good day?" the answer is likely a garbled, "Yeah." An open invitation such as, "Tell me something funny that happened during lunch," likely results in a detailed report of Zack laughing so hard that his noodle soup came out of his nose. Now that's conversation to warm a parent's heart!

What Parents **Really** Do

As usual, Sondra came home and I casually said, "Tell me something interesting about your day." She complained, "It was a bad day at school." I had her do a reality check. We listed, hour by hour, what her day had been like since she woke up. The start of the list looked like this:

7:30   *Mom made me French toast*
8:30   *Mrs. Johnson let me lead the flag salute*
9:30   *Had fun playing dodgeball in PE*
10:30 *Got an A on my spelling test*
11:30 *Dropped bag of chips on the floor*
12:30 *Got to pick the book for story time*

Instead of a "bad day," she saw that she had a "bad three minutes" when she dropped her chips. Now she says, "I had a great day . . . all except for a few bad minutes, Mom."

Silvana

Traditional Parenting Tip

To help your children learn responsibility, have them experience the law of cause and effect. As adults, if we fail to meet a work deadline, for example, natural (and usually negative) consequences occur. If your daughter leaves her soccer shoes outdoors on a rainy day, they'll probably be wet the next time she needs to wear them. Rather than buying a new pair of shoes or rushing to dry them for her, a simple statement like "Soccer shoes stay dry if they are kept in the garage" teaches a lesson. Parents often are too quick to rescue their children from what could be a learning experience.

What Parents **Really** <u>Do</u>

My fifth-grade son was constantly forgetting his lunch, his homework, or his saxophone. I'd remind him and set his things in front of the door. Nothing worked. At least once a week, he'd call from school with a desperate voice and say, "Pleeeeeeease Mom . . . can you bring my lunch? I promise never to forget it again. This is the very last time you'll have to bring it to me. Pleeeeeeease?" Against my better judgment, I'd drive to the school with the forgotten item.

One day, after getting yet another pleading call, I took the forgotten lunch sack and decorated it. I added two large balloons to the top, hung pink streamers from the bottom of the bag, and wrote his name in glitter on the side. For extra effect I used a bold marker and wrote, "Mom loves you" over the entire sack. It was a gaudy, colorful masterpiece. The school secretary gladly delivered it to him with a flourish in front of the entire class.

He never forgot another school item again.

Cynthia Johanson, former preschool teacher

Paying for Mom's Taxi Service

Traditional Parenting Tip

Parents often feel they are running a free taxi service for their children. Soccer, music classes, and play dates all require coordination of transportation details. Enlist older children's help by asking them to post their schedules on a master calendar. It then becomes their responsibility to inform you of their pickup and drop-off needs ahead of time.

What Parents **Really** Do

I was tired of my children expecting me to drop everything or even rearrange my work schedule in order to take them someplace. I came up with this plan: They got two "free" trips per week. I'd take them to basketball practice or to a friend's house. After that, if they wanted to go someplace else, I calculated my driving time, and they owed me an equal amount of time by doing chores. A trip to the mall? Sure! That's thirty minutes of my time. As soon as they completed thirty minutes of vacuuming the car or sweeping the garage, I'd take them to the mall. They soon started to respect the time I spent driving because they saw how much time it took for them to do chores.

Marion Webster

Kmart or Designer Labels?

Traditional Parenting Tip

Listen to your children when they insist they need the latest name-brand shirt or pair of shoes. Children want to feel like a part of their peer group, so help them find ways to earn the money to buy the coveted item. If their must-have shoes cost ninety dollars and you are willing to buy a comparable pair for forty dollars, have them pay the remaining fifty dollars themselves. They'll get the item they want, but they'll learn it takes effort to buy the higher-priced item.

What Parents Really Do

My thirteen-year-old insisted the reason she wanted name-brand clothing was because it was higher quality and lasted longer. She claimed the logo wasn't important to her . . . just that the item was made well.

To test her theory, I purchased a name-brand, blue striped blouse for thirty-eight dollars. Then I drove to Kmart and bought a similar blue striped blouse for nine dollars. Painstakingly, I removed the label from the back neck of each blouse and sewed the Kmart tag onto the designer label blouse and vice versa. After wrapping both blouses, I presented both to my daughter, saying, "I wasn't sure which one you liked best, so I bought two. We can return the one you don't like." The instant she saw the designer label, my daughter fell in love with that blouse, wearing it twice a week for over a month. Finally I couldn't stand it any longer and told her the truth. She had been wearing a Kmart blouse! We had a good laugh and she saw how labels do influence young teens' opinions.

Allan Clark, amateur tailor

Traditional Parenting Tip

When asking children to do something, give clear directions. Saying, "Please pick up the dirty clothes in your room and make your bed," produces better results than saying, "This room is a mess. Clean it!" If children have specific tasks, it's easier for them to follow through and accomplish what they are supposed to do. Setting an egg timer or saying, "Your books need to be back on the bookshelf in ten minutes" is a specific direction children can follow.

What Parents **Really** Do

I would give my son specific directions to take out the trash or walk the dog. He'd always answer with, "In just a minute, after I finish this computer game," or "I forgot. I'm really sorry." One day he called from school, asking me to pick him up because he'd missed the bus. I told him I'd be there in ten minutes. Instead of getting in the car, I called the principal to let him know about my plan. Twenty minutes later, my son called again. Very innocently, I told him I'd forgotten because I was busy doing laundry but would come right away. Another twenty minutes passed and my son called to see where I was. "Oh, I'm so sorry! I forgot! I was so involved in my magazine. Don't worry, I'm on my way!" I told him. Another twenty minutes passed. When I answered the phone, my son said, "Okay, Mom! I get the point. Please come get me and I'll be more responsible about my chores." I was so elated I only made him wait another fifteen minutes before I picked him up.

Bev Swanson

Whiners Never Win

Traditional Parenting Tip

Moooommmm, I don't waaaaant to cleeeeannn my rooooom." The sound of a child's whining voice can send shivers down an adult's spine. Sometimes we give in to their demands simply to stop the whining. The next time your children whine over a minor complaint, take time to look them directly in the eye. Ask them, "Please repeat what you just said, exactly how you said it." As they hear their whiny statement again, they often understand they were whining. Then ask them to repeat the sentence in a positive way without whining.

What Parents **Really** Do

I don't tolerate whining well at all! When my boys were toddlers and in an especially whiny stage, I simply stopped them midsentence if they approached me for something in a whiny voice and said, "I'm sorry, I can't hear you when you whine. My ears don't work. I'm setting the timer for one minute, and when it beeps, you may speak to me again about this in a normal tone of voice." When the timer went off, nine times out of ten, the boys would approach me and ask in an appropriate manner. Occasionally, I had to set the timer a second or third time if they were having a tough day in the whining department! Although they are now nine and six, and for the most part over the whining stage, there are still days when the timer gets set. It works!

Laura Sabin Riley, author of *All Mothers Are Working Mothers* and *The ABC's of Character*

Band-Aids Work Miracles

Traditional Parenting Tip

Many traditional parenting books stress the importance of rationalizing, explaining, and dialoguing with children. In some situations, forget the lengthy conversations. You're the adult. It isn't necessary to come up with a twelve-point discussion list about the need to brush teeth before bed. Simply repeat, "Time to brush your teeth." If your kids stall and argue, you simply repeat, "Time to brush your teeth." They soon get tired of your repetitive statement.

What Parents **Really** Do

I tried without success to get my two-year-old to stop nursing. I did everything the parenting books said, like giving her a cup, not holding her close, distracting her. She wanted to nurse! Reasoning with her, giving lengthy explanations of her new baby sister arriving, had little effect. One day I put two Band-Aids on my nipples. When she came up to nurse, I showed her the Band-Aids and said, "Sorry, they're broken. No milk." She checked in three more times before giving up nursing for good.

> Mom with three kids (Do you really
> think I'd reveal my name?)

Kids *Can* Do It

Traditional Parenting Tip

You wouldn't expect a twelve-year-old to drive a car, yet children should show responsibility in many areas of their lives. Evaluate all *your* actions. Are you doing things your children could do? If they want to go to the movies, do they look up the playing schedule? Are you filling out your ten-year-old's application for summer camp? Why can't she fill it out herself (with you checking it over, of course)? Did he buy an item of clothing that didn't fit? Let him explain to the clerk why it needs to be exchanged.

What Parents **Really** Do

My twelve-year-old son needed new tennis shoes. Of course, he wanted the newest, the coolest, and the most expensive pair. He even offered to chip in twenty dollars of his own money. I told him to call three different stores to check on the price of the shoes, plus ask if a sale was coming up. He refused. I said, "You expect me to pay the majority of the shoes and drive you to the mall. This requires some effort from you. When I see a written record of the calls you made and the prices they quoted, I'll take you to buy the shoes." It took three weeks before he called the stores.

Mom and insurance agent

Taxis Teach Responsibility

Traditional Parenting Tip

Parents want to make things easy for their children. We cajole them to eat nutritious foods and clean up their messes. While it makes us feel good, it does little to help children learn responsibility. Children develop resilient personalities by solving problems and overcoming age-appropriate difficulties. Role-play with children to give them confidence about what to say in certain situations. If they think a teacher graded their essay test unfairly, help them figure out what to say to the teacher. Rather than solving all their problems for them, teach skills so children can learn to solve their own problems.

What Parents **Really** Do

My twelve-year-old daughter was consistently late for school. I'd drive her—grumbling and lecturing the entire way, of course. I realized she was old enough to take responsibility for herself. One afternoon, over a cup of tea, I calmly explained the new system. If she missed the bus, I would call a taxi to take her to school . . . and she'd pay for it. We even drove to the bank and had her withdraw twenty-five dollars from her savings account so she'd have cash on hand. Sure enough, two days later, she missed the bus. She ended up paying eighteen dollars for the taxicab and was thoroughly humiliated to arrive at school in a bright yellow taxi.

Mom in Cleveland

Singing through the SATs

Traditional Parenting Tip

Think back to when you were in third grade. Did your mother help you do your homework? Then why are you helping your daughter? Children need proper tools to study. They don't need an adult doing the work for them. Work out a schedule for homework. Do they do better if they get playtime before studying? Some children actually prefer to get their homework done first. This gives them a feeling of freedom as they play. Provide a quiet place to study complete with sharpened pencils and extra paper. You provide encouragement; they provide the effort. Sometimes it helps to have an adult sit with children, paying bills or reading to help the kids shift into a study mode. After a few minutes, walk away so your children learn to work independently. Of course you'll be readily available with an encyclopedia when they shout, "Mom, what's the main export of Madagascar?"

What Parents **Really** Do

My daughter had difficulty reading long paragraphs from her social studies or history textbooks. When reviewing for a test, we'd all sit in a circle and play "Singing Sillies." The idea was to "sing" the words we were reading from her textbook. Any tune was appropriate. (You've never studied the Civil War until you've sung about it with an operatic flair.) We'd take turns at each paragraph, singing out facts and statistics. This provided a low-stress yet effective way for her to review the necessary material.

Tone-deaf mom

Parents, Not Best Friends

Traditional Parenting Tip

You love your children intensely. No wonder you want them to like you. Yet you are the adult, the parent. Your years of experience give you wisdom to make tough decisions. Parents often want to be buddies with their children, but this gives your child a false sense of security. He may be in for a surprise when other adults don't treat him as an equal. Make it clear, in a loving way, that you and your child are not on equal terms.

What Parents **Really** Do

This is what I told each of my children when they yelled, "I hate you!" as so many kids do at least once. "Your job as a child, at one time or another, is to hate your parents. This is natural. My job is to give you the tools to do your job effectively. Consider my refusal to be my way of making sure you are doing your job." In the face of such sarcasm, all they could do was walk away.

Carmen Leal, author of *Portraits of Huntington's*

Rules for Success

Traditional Parenting Tip

Elementary school teachers frequently complain about their students' lack of respect for everyday rules. Students challenge the reason for walking in the halls or listening attentively as others speak. Teach your children the importance of thinking about other people's feelings. Ask questions such as: "What would happen if everyone just grabbed the pieces of pizza all at once?" "How could we make sure the new neighbor girl feels welcome?" Point out how rules of common courtesy help make life more enjoyable for everyone.

What Parents **Really** Do

I'm embarrassed to admit this activity we occasionally do. After buying a ticket for a movie or a play, I like to see if I can "sneak in" without giving up my ticket to the ticket taker. (Hey, I did pay for the ticket, so it's totally legitimate!) There's a certain thrill in walking in with a large group, avoiding eye contact with the ticket taker, and then announcing, "I did it!" upon reaching the theater door. My daughter and I love doing this while my husband and son ignore us totally. They walk up to the ticket taker and loudly proclaim, "Here are our tickets to see the movie." They act as if we are committing a major crime.

Not willing to give my name!

Dealing with a "Perfect" Child

Traditional Parenting Tip

As parents, we want our children to learn respect for rules and authority. Teaching respect is an ongoing process beginning with a toddler's screaming demands for another cookie. Model positive behavior. Let your child watch you and an older sibling act out the respectful way to ask for a cookie. When your child is calm, discuss the importance of showing respect and consideration for others.

What Parents **Really** Do

I confess—all my life I've pushed the limits to the maximum breaking point. So how did I end up with a daughter who is thoughtful, considerate, and obedient? Trina was a model child and it drove me crazy! She followed all the rules at home and school. I repeatedly told her, "Before you graduate from high school, you *have* to skip at least one class. I want you to feel that adrenaline rush that comes from breaking a rule." She was horrified at the thought, but I insisted she skip a class. One day I got a call from Trina at school. In a hushed voice, she said, "Mom—I can't believe I'm doing this! I'm so scared! I'm skipping class!" I was so proud of my risk-taking daughter. Naturally, this idea works only if you have a child that consistently follows rules. Giving some children "permission" to skip class could result in a spotty attendance record!

Silvana

Conclusion

Let's face it. Some of you reading this book will shake your heads incredulously and say, "I can't believe that mother did that! How can parents be so crazy? I could never do that!" Yet others of you are saying, "What a great idea! I can't wait until my son complains about dinner. I'll serve him rice all weekend!" Every one of us has different parenting styles, and we can all learn from each other. If your nagging doesn't seem to be working in getting your daughter to clean her room, maybe a different technique is in order. Yes, it may seem severe to remove all her clothes for a week, but perhaps that's the "drastic" measure needed to have an impact on her.

The parents in this book love their children and want the best for them. Sometimes "the best" means trying untraditional parenting ideas. Our daughter Sondra has always been a night owl. We tried everything we could to get her to go to bed at a "normal" time. Nothing worked. We saw she simply did not need as much sleep as her weary middle-aged parents. Now, she tucks *us* into bed and goes to her room. Sometimes at 11:00 P.M. we hear her singing Broadway show tunes or rearranging bedroom furniture. The next morning she wakes up with a big smile and even more energy than the day before. In this case, forcing her to be in bed at 8:30 would only lead to frustration.

I hope this book has given you new ideas about how to deal with your children in a variety of situations. Instead of getting frustrated, get creative! Take your cue from other parents and try some of their techniques. Maybe their experiences are just what you need to help get you through a difficult situation. The next time you feel unappreciated, go on strike! Put on disguises and follow them on their trip to the mall. And if your children have trouble getting to bed at night, offer to hang their stuffed animals from the ceiling fan!

Silvana Clark, wife of Allan and mother of two daughters, is the author of ten books and numerous articles. She was a recreation supervisor for ten years and is presently a professional speaker. She has appeared on *The 700 Club* and *Home Matters*. Silvana has given presentations for the International Women's Conference and the Crystal Cathedral, and at conferences across the country. Presently she and her family are taking a year-long trip around the United States in an RV. Silvana and her youngest daughter, Sondra, were selected as an "inspirational team" to carry the Olympic torch. When not on the road, Silvana and her family live in Bellingham, Washington.